A STUDENT'S GUIDE TO ACING COLLEGE

Tips, Tools, and Strategies for Academic Success

Jeffrey Vaske

iUniverse, Inc.
Bloomington

A Student's Guide to Acing College
Tips, Tools, and Strategies for Academic Success

iUniverse books may be ordered through booksellers or by contacting:

iUniverse
1663 Liberty Drive
Bloomington, IN 47403
www.iuniverse.com
1-800-Authors (1-800-288-4677)

ISBN: 978-1-4620-0120-0 (pbk)
ISBN: 978-1-4620-0121-7 (cloth)
ISBN: 978-1-4620-0122-4 (ebk)

Library of Congress Control Number: 2011903167

Printed in the United States of America

Cover photo courtesy of Grand View University, Des Moines, Iowa.
Author photo taken by Tim Vorland Photography, Des Moines, Iowa.
Fallen Soldier Tribute and Prayer of Thanksgiving images designed by Noah Judson.

iUniverse rev. date: 3/18/2011

To my beautiful wife, Jeannine,
who is a constant source
of love, support, and inspiration.

Contents

Introduction

Imagine that it is welcome weekend for incoming freshmen at your college, and you have just finished moving into your dorm room or apartment. You say good-bye to your loved ones, and they begin to leave. The door closes, and after a few minutes it hits you for the first time: you are on your own, facing a monumental challenge. You must spend the next several years of your life earning a college degree.

Your heart begins to race, and the anxiety and uncertainty of the unknown start to take over. What are my classes going to be like? Will I have good instructors? Will I have to write a lot of papers? Will the tests be difficult? Will I perform as well as the other students? Will I be able to get all of my homework done while juggling school, work, and a social life? Will I successfully complete my degree so that I can get a good job and not disappoint my loved ones? Will I ...? Will I ...? Will I ...?

Slow down, take a deep breath, and relax! This is a very common reaction to have during the first few days of your college experience. Moreover, these questions are all valid and relevant, especially when pondering the many uncertainties that accompany being a college freshman. However, luck and good fortune are on your side because fate has bestowed a copy of this book upon you.

You might have acquired this book in one of several different ways: 1) it might have been a high school graduation gift; 2) you might have seen it in the campus bookstore and thought that it would be a wise investment; or 3) it might be required reading for one of your freshman seminar or introductory courses. Regardless of how you came to possess this book, I can assure you that you will not be disappointed. If utilized properly, the tips, tools, and strategies in the forthcoming chapters will serve as the foundation to your academic success in college.

At this point, you might be second-guessing yourself and your ability to do well in college. Sure, you were a good—or perhaps even a great—student in high school, but this is college! It is a completely different ballgame, right?

Well, the answer is both yes and no. Of course, college academics are almost always more rigorous than high school academics, but the fundamental skills needed to master academics at any level remain constant. The key to success at the next level though, is to sharpen those fundamental skills and add a few new ones that are unique to the college experience. In doing so, you will be fully prepared to make a smooth transition into college academics.

In this book, I will show you the path to academic success in college. I will present numerous tips, tools, and strategies that will help you improve your fundamental academic skills. Furthermore, I will introduce you to many resources that are unique to the college experience, which will assist you in achieving the grades that you desire. My hope is that you will use the information in this book as a blueprint of sorts to build a solid foundation so that you can achieve total academic success in college.

Right about now, you might be wondering, "Okay, who is this author, and what are his credentials for writing such a book?" This is a completely legitimate question, so please allow me to introduce myself.

My name is Jeffrey Vaske, and I graduated from Grand View University in 2007 with a Bachelor of Science in Nursing and a Bachelor of Arts in History. I completed 209 undergraduate college credit hours and graduated Summa Cum Laude with a perfect 4.0 GPA. I was named to the President's List ten consecutive semesters, received numerous academic awards, and was a member of several academic honor societies. I achieved all of this while also participating in a very demanding Army Reserve

Officer Training Corps (ROTC) program. Since finishing my undergraduate degrees, I have also completed twelve graduate credit hours at Texas A&M University and have maintained a 4.0 GPA there as well.

I am not a genius by any stretch of the imagination, and I certainly do not have a photographic memory. Nevertheless, I achieved complete academic success in college by developing, fine-tuning, and implementing a systematic approach to academics that I would like to share with you in this book. I was inspired to write this book because I believe that any student, when equipped with the proper tools, can reach and exceed all of his or her academic goals. In my humble opinion, college is just a giant game of chess: if you employ a solid strategy and always remain focused on your goals, you will dominate the game.

Clearly, there are numerous books about college success on the market today, so what makes this one different from any of the others? First of all, most of the other books were written by authors who are much older and have a master's or a doctoral degree. Indeed, I do not have a doctoral or even a master's degree yet, but that is precisely what sets me apart from many of the authors who have already written on this subject.

Many of these authors do not view college academics entirely through the eyes of today's contemporary student. Moreover, some authors even fail to present their information in an accessible way so that students can get the information they need quickly. In the end, the authors' failure to connect with today's student population prevents the students from applying the information presented to their education.

The reason that many authors are unable to relate to modern students and their experiences as college freshmen in today's academic world is because they are years and years removed from their own undergraduate educations. They usually write to students based upon their assumed "authority" as a master's- or doctoral-prepared individual rather than someone who was just recently in your shoes. Certainly, a higher level of education adds credibility to some extent, but how can they possibly relate to what you are going through?

I started writing this book in 2008 when I was only twenty-four years old, just eighteen months after completing my undergraduate degrees. Hence, I am essentially writing to you on a peer-to-peer level, which most of the other authors cannot say for themselves. The result is a much more user-friendly and relevant work that will assist you greatly in your endeavors to succeed in college academics, written by someone who was literally in your shoes just a short time ago.

Two other major distinctions between this work and many of the others that are currently on the market are focus and length. This book focuses solely on academics and the things that you can do to set yourself up for success. I do not digress heavily into the social aspects of college, nor do I attempt to cover every possible facet of the college experience. My intent is to set you up for academic success and to help you develop strong skills that will serve you well both in college and in life.

Finally, most of the books about college success on the market today are quite lengthy. In fact, many of them are several hundred pages long. Once again, this is where other authors lose touch with reality. As a college student, you will already have plenty of reading to do for your classes. You do not need another three or four hundred pages tacked onto your workload. That is why, when I set out to write this book, I specifically aimed to keep it less than one hundred pages in length. My goal was and is to present quality information in an efficient and timely manner.

In the chapters that follow, I will outline a step-by-step plan of attack to ensure that you do not waste your time, efforts, and perhaps most important, your money (or your parents' money) on failed attempts to succeed in college academics. I will present various tips, tools, and strategies that can be utilized to improve your weaknesses or supplement your existing strengths as a student. Whether you choose to follow the advice in this book in its entirety or to simply pick up a few new pointers along the way, I can assure you that the time you invest in reading this book will be well spent.

Having said that, I do understand that all students begin their college experience with various academic strengths and weaknesses. I also realize that students come from all walks of life and that different things work for different people. Consequently, I am not trying to impress upon you that the *only* way to succeed in college academics is to adhere to the following tips, tools, and strategies exactly as they are presented. On the contrary, I am merely attempting to expose you to the many different resources that you can draw upon to maximize your potential for academic success in college.

After all, with the rising costs associated with higher education today and the amount of time and energy you will spend earning your degree, you owe it to yourself to do the very best you can. Years down the road, I want you to be able to reflect upon your college experience and say that you have no regrets about your academic performance. Accordingly, my goal is to help make you a better student so that you can graduate and take that next big step in your life. Whether it is landing that first job after graduation or continuing your education in graduate school, achieving academic success in college will open unlimited doors for you. With hard work and determination, you will be able to write your own ticket in life and before you know it, will begin to achieve all of your dreams!

So sit back, set your mind at ease, and enjoy the read.
You are well on your way to academic success!

Jeffrey Vaske

CHAPTER 1:

You Do Not Have to Be a Genius

A common misconception is that you have to be extraordinarily intelligent to achieve academic success in college. Some people might say that this accomplishment requires a photographic memory or a natural writing ability that puts one well above his or her peers. Certainly, both of these qualities help. However, for the vast majority of students, these abilities just do not exist. So let me be the first to tell you that you do not have to be a genius to achieve academic success in college.

You are probably thinking to yourself, "Sure, you might not be a genius or have a photographic memory, but you probably got a 33 on your ACT or a 2200 on your SAT." Once again, not true in my case. I took the ACT three times, and the highest score I earned was a 25, with an average score of 23.3. This score is nothing special and identifies me as being about average, so I must be an average student, right? Wrong again. I, and I am sure many other students along the way, have long felt that the standardized tests that colleges use to evaluate students for admission (i.e., the ACT and SAT) are flawed.

First of all, some students are simply not good at taking tests, especially when it comes to standardized tests. Standardized tests cover a broad range of material related to general topics like reading, science, and math. Even though I took preparatory courses and went over hundreds of practice questions, I found it very difficult to study for and do well on standardized tests. On the other hand, if given a pretty good idea of what to study, I could always prepare myself well enough to succeed on classroom tests as they related to specific course material.

The other issue I have with standardized tests is that many people falsely believe that they are a measure of intelligence. In reality, they are a measurement of one's educational development, not one's intellegence.[1] Certainly some students are, by either nature or nurture, smarter than others and will score higher on standardized tests. However, what do you (and all other students) do when you do not know the answer to a particular question? You test the laws of probability and guess, hoping that luck will be on your side.

Now I do not know about you, but I can honestly say that I guessed on about 40 percent of the questions each time that I took the ACT. I am sure that I answered a few of those questions correctly, but the laws of probability would dictate that I answered the majority of them incorrectly. The only reason I raised my ACT score from a 21 to a 24 and then from a 24 to a 25 on the third attempt was probably because I just guessed a little better each time. So do not get discouraged if you did not score well on the ACT or SAT. They are not a true measure of your intelligence.

Finally and perhaps most noteworthy, is that standardized tests are not predictors of academic success. This is a tough pill to swallow for some admissions counselors who turn away very capable students every year due to low test scores on the ACT or SAT. In fact, I was discriminated against during my college application process because I only scored a 25 on the ACT. Reality check: just because someone scores a 33 on the ACT or a 2200 on the SAT, it does not guarantee that he or she will succeed in college academics. Certainly, there must be a process for colleges to evaluate potential students before admitting them, but I challenge all admissions counselors to focus less on these numbers and more on the individual profiles of each prospective student.

As I will discuss throughout this book, achieving academic success in college involves much more than simply scoring well on a standardized test. Academic success is achieved by constantly developing, improving, and properly utilizing a multitude of skills over the course of one's college career. Indeed, a student might have scored a 33 on their ACT, but he or she must still possess strong organizational and time management skills. That person must also 1) go to class every day, 2) establish sound relationships with their instructors, 3) practice good study habits, 4) improve his or her test-taking abilities, 5) work to become a proficient writer, 6) understand the dynamics of group projects, and 7) exploit valuable campus resources.

In conclusion, you do not have to be a genius to achieve academic success in college. Even if your high school grades were not the greatest or you scored low on the ACT or SAT, it does not mean that you cannot succeed at the highest level in college academics. Furthermore, do not let these perceived shortcomings deter you from pursuing a particular field of study or the profession that you desire most in life.

If you want to become a pharmacist, a lawyer, a teacher, a nurse, or anything else that your heart desires, pursue that goal with all of your might. Do not let *anyone* tell you what you can or cannot do, and do not settle for anything less than what you want. Finally, remember that college is a marathon, not a sprint, and that you must develop the right frame of mind to make it to the finish line.

Key Points:

- You do not have to be a genius to achieve academic success in college.

- Do not dwell upon standardized test scores: the ACT and SAT are not predictors of academic success.

- Do not settle for anything less than what you want in life.

CHAPTER 2:

Mind Over Matter

With a goal of obtaining your associate's, bachelor's, master's, or doctoral degree, the thought of spending the next several years of your life working toward a college degree can be very overwhelming. You might feel as if you are a hiker standing at the base of a large mountain, looking straight up at the peak. That peak is your goal and in this case, your goal is to earn a college degree.

The distance you must traverse to reach that goal will be long and difficult. Still, you must keep things in perspective and remain focused on the present. A very wise man once told me, "You cannot control the past and you cannot control the future, but you can control the present. So do not dwell upon the past and do not worry about the future. Focus on what you can control. Focus on the present."[2]

The moral of the story is that you should remain focused on the present day, not the *should have*s of yesterday or the *what ifs* of tomorrow. Dwelling upon past events and contemplating potential future events will only make you more anxious in the present, which will negatively affect your performance in the present. Consequently, the strategy here is to set small, everyday goals that will help you achieve your mid- and long-term goals.

For example, sit down on Sunday evening and make a list of goals that you want to accomplish during the upcoming week. Likewise, when you get up each morning, take a moment to make a list of goals that you want to accomplish for that particular day. Consider any upcoming deadlines related to papers, projects, or tests, and prioritize your lists according to what must be completed first. Focusing on and achieving these little goals will do several things for you, both in terms of getting your work completed and in terms of attaining the right frame of mind to "climb the mountain."

First, it will help you stay focused on the present and will prevent your mind from anguishing about the past or the future. Remaining focused on the present will minimize your anxiety and therefore increase your productivity. Second, it will give you a sense of accomplishment each day as you systematically cross items off of your to-do list. This sense of accomplishment will give you valuable confidence in yourself and in your abilities to perform at the college-level. Finally, making daily and weekly lists of goals will help you adequately prioritize your work to get it completed on time. This will ensure that you are always well prepared for class and for any tests or projects that you might have during each week.

Making daily and weekly lists of goals will also assist you in achieving your overall goals for each semester and each academic year. You will discover that each semester builds upon one another and that the habits you develop early on will set the tone for your entire academic career. Being mindful of this is particularly important if you are in an associate's degree program and want to eventually get into a bachelor's degree program or if you are in a bachelor's program and want to ultimately get into a graduate or professional program (e.g., medical, dental, or law school). In order to achieve these things, it is imperative that you set short-, mid-, and long-term academic goals along the way.

Setting goals and remaining focused on the present are essential in achieving the psychological edge needed to "run the marathon" that is college academics. Once again, failing to do these things will only increase your anxiety and promote poor academic performance. Thus, I would argue that controlling your anxiety is one of the most important aspects of achieving academic success in college.

Even so, what is anxiety, exactly? There are numerous definitions for **anxiety**, but it is generally understood to be a fear of the unknown. In other words, it is apprehension about the future caused by the uncertainties of the present. Hence, in order to control, alleviate, and eventually eliminate anxiety altogether, you must first identify your fears and then take the necessary steps to prevent those fears from controlling your life.

In the end, you must understand the power of mind over matter. You, and you alone, can eliminate your anxiety with your actions: remain focused on the present, and set daily/weekly goals in order to achieve your short-, mid-, and long-term academic goals. As we will discuss in the next chapter, the key to achieving these goals is to get organized so that you are prepared for whatever comes your way. After all, in academics as in life, chance favors those who are well prepared!

Key Points:

- Always remain focused on the present: do not dwell upon the past and do not worry about the future.

- Set daily and weekly goals in order to achieve your short-, mid-, and long-term academic goals.

- Strive to minimize your anxiety so that you can maximize your productivity.

CHAPTER 3:
Live an Organized Life

In the chaos and turmoil of our modern world, one of the most difficult things to do is to achieve some level of organization so that you can function normally on a daily basis. Perhaps the term *normal* ceases to have meaning in our advanced society with all of its distractions: cell phones, televisions, video games, computers, MP3 players, and so forth. Still, as a college student (particularly as a college freshman), one of the best things you can do to ensure academic success is to sort through all of these distractions. In other words, get organized: attain a level of structure that works best for you and that will set you up for success.

As a college student, you will have numerous commitments to keep and deadlines to meet. Accordingly, one of the most powerful weapons in the college student's arsenal is the academic planner. As you will soon find out, this handy little device will become your lifeline for staying organized on a day-to-day basis throughout your college career. Most notably, it will help you develop and adhere to a productive schedule.

You can usually purchase an annual academic planner from the college bookstore for less than five dollars (compared to the cost of your books, this is a drop in the bucket). Also, some colleges make deals with publishing companies to create individualized academic planners for their particular institutions. The value here is that key dates specific to your institution (e.g., holidays, scheduled breaks, midterms, and finals) will already be noted in the planner for each semester, which is a nice feature.

In light of today's technology, one might argue that a smart phone or some other electronic device is a much better choice for staying organized. If that is the case for you, then by all means use whatever fits your individual needs and preferences. The key point, however, is that you should use some method or tool to stay organized throughout the semester. Once you decide what that method is, be sure to keep a detailed record of the following: 1) class times and locations; 2) dates for all tests; and 3) deadlines for all assignments, such as readings, papers, and projects. It is also essential to highlight any holidays or scheduled breaks during the semester so that you can plan well in advance to get your work completed on time.

At the beginning of every semester, each of your instructors will give you a syllabus for his or her course. Each course syllabus will vary slightly but should include most, if not all, of the following: 1) the course description, 2) the desired course outcomes, 3) the guidelines for classroom conduct, 4) the policies for tardiness/absence, 5) the grading scale, and 6) the course schedule or timeline, which will identify all important dates and deadlines. Also, if there are papers or projects required in the course, the syllabus will likely describe them in some detail.

After receiving each syllabus, the very first thing that you should do is highlight all pertinent dates or deadlines and then record them in your academic planner. Likewise, at the end of each class session, record any assignments or deadlines for the next time that particular course meets. Doing these basic things will ensure that you are always organized and well prepared for each and every class session.

Getting and maintaining an academic planner of some sort is certainly the easiest and best way to stay organized throughout each semester. Nonetheless, you must also possess the means and ability to manage your notes and paperwork from each course. This is best accomplished by having separate folders and notebooks for each individual course. Though, keep it simple and purchase a five-in-one binder or notebook. Multi-ring binders and notebooks are a great way to keep all of your notes separate yet organized in one convenient location. They are usually large enough to get you through the entire semester and have areas where you can store and organize paperwork from each course alongside your notes.

When taking notes, it is a good idea to date each entry for every individual class session and clearly identify when new chapters or units begin. This will greatly assist you when you go back to study for tests. Also, it is helpful to use different colors of ink when taking notes on paper. For instance, if your course meets on Monday, Wednesday, and Friday, you could take in blue ink on Monday, green ink on Wednesday, and black ink on Friday. This will help keep your notes for each class session visibly separated by both date and time, as well as by content, which will further assist you when you study.

On the other hand, many students prefer to type class notes on a laptop computer. If this is your preference, then organizing your notes from each class session will be quite easy, as you can bold or italicize entries and separate content as needed. You can also format your notes to fit the needs of each individual course and then print off the notes later to study for tests. In either case, the importance of taking good notes cannot be overstated.

In terms of course-related documents, always keep the syllabus for each course readily available, perhaps on top of all the other papers and handouts for that course. This will force you to look at it frequently, which will constantly remind you of any deadlines and allow you to cross off assignments as you complete them. In addition, it is a good idea to date the papers and handouts that you receive in each course, and highlight all pertinent information to aid you when you prepare to write papers or study for tests.

These are just a few tips and strategies to assist you with organization during the academic year. I realize that some people really struggle with organization, but you must understand and accept the fact that it is a major key to achieving academic success in college. It might not be all that exciting and some of your friends might tease you about your efforts to stay organized, but you will have the last laugh. When your friends are trying to locate lecture notes from week three the night before the midterm, you will be able to flip right to that page of your notebook and share (or not share) the notes with them.

Ultimately, your academic success will hinge on your abilities to get and remain organized throughout each semester. Yet you must also realize how vitally important it is to go to class. What? You have to actually go to class in college? What a novel concept! Indeed, you do. Besides, you will not be able to share your neatly organized notes from week three with your friends if you were not in class to write them down in the first place!

Key Points:

- Sort through the daily distractions of life and develop a structured schedule in order to achieve a high level of organization.

- Obtain and utilize an academic planner on a daily basis.

- Maintain a separate folder and notebook for each course, and file all course materials chronologically.

- Review each course syllabus on a regular basis to ensure that you stay ahead of all assignments and deadlines.

Chapter 4:

Go to Class (and Apply Yourself)

Students in contemporary society face a multitude of distractions that often prevent them from attending class, particularly on Fridays because the temptation to start the weekend early is just too irresistible to pass up. Nonetheless (and this might sound like a no-brainer), but you actually have to go to class to succeed in college academics! Still, if you will not listen to me, perhaps you will listen to your wallet. Money definitely talks, and when it comes to college expenses, it screams!

College is a tremendously expensive endeavor at any and every level, especially when you add up the costs of the following: 1) tuition, 2) room and board, 3) books, 4) supplies, 5) applicable fees, 6) transportation, and 7) other miscellaneous personal expenses. The sum of all college-related expenses for any given semester is astronomical, and someone is paying that bill. Although some students live in a bubble because they are on scholarship or because their parents are supporting them, the vast majority of students in this country are responsible for their own college expenses.

In fact, nearly two-thirds (66 percent) of college freshmen have concerns about being able to finance their education.[3] If you fall into this category, it is crucial that you avoid throwing money away by skipping classes. Skipping classes can cost you a hefty sum of money. To illustrate my point, let us calculate the direct cost of skipping just *one* class.

Let us assume that you are attending a four-year state school and that your total expenses for one semester equal $10,000 (a conservative estimate assuming that your tuition, books, supplies, and fees cost about $4,000 and that your room and board, transportation, and other personal expenses cost about $6,000). Let us also assume that you are taking twelve credit hours, which is the minimum number of hours required to be considered a full-time student at most colleges. A schedule with twelve credit hours usually translates into four, three-credit hour courses. The average course meets for a one-hour class session three times per week for fifteen weeks during the semester (not including finals week).

This equates to a total of 180 class sessions that you could possibly attend throughout the semester. So, take $10,000 and divide it by 180. This demonstrates that each individual class session costs you $55.55, whether you attend it or not. Thus, every time you skip a class (regardless of the reason), you are throwing away $55.55!

Now, this scenario may not reflect your individual situation exactly, but I challenge you to plug in your own numbers and calculate precisely how much it costs you every time you skip a class. For most students, the reality that they are wasting such a large amount of money each time they skip a class probably does not register because almost all college expenses have to be paid in full at the beginning of every semester. In other words, the money is out of sight and out of mind. However, if you actually had to shell out $55.55 every time you entered or failed to enter a classroom, it would make you absolutely sick! So you might think twice about wanting to start your weekend early by skipping all of your Friday classes.

With all considerations of money aside, I am sure you have heard the legendary tale of the student who skipped class all semester, only showed up to take the tests, and still managed to get a C or D to pass the course. First, this rarely (if ever) actually happens in real life. Second, getting a C or D just to pass a course is nothing to brag about, especially when a little time and effort can easily earn you an A or a B.

Once again, going to class is absolutely essential if you want to succeed in college academics and, perhaps more important, become proficient in your field of study. After all, it is very difficult to learn anything if you never attend class. Furthermore, attendance is often counted as part of your overall grade, and missing several class sessions throughout the semester will adversely affect your final grade for the course.

Even so, simply going to class does not automatically guarantee that you will do well in the course. You have to know how to apply yourself while you are in class to maximize learning and facilitate your mastery of the course material. Consequently, in the rest of this chapter, I will outline a few important things to consider once you get to class. Specifically, the appropriate classroom engagement that will help you get the most out of each and every class session that you attend.

Up to this point, we have established how important it is to go to class, and hopefully you have decided to make every effort to attend all of your class sessions. This starts first and foremost by being punctual (even early) for each class session, which will ensure that you do not miss any course material. Additionally, instructors tend to make important announcements at the beginning of each class session regarding assignments, papers, and tests, so you certainly do not want to be absent for that information.

Moreover, neither instructors nor students appreciate classroom interruptions, and arriving late to class is both a visible and auditory interruption. In the eyes of the instructor, your failure to arrive on time to class conveys a lack of respect for both that instructor and for your fellow students. Therefore, do yourself and your grade a big favor, and arrive on time for each class session. Doing so will give you the best chance for success and will also help you to establish sound relationships with your instructors (more on this in Chapter 5, "Establish a Good Rapport with Your Instructors").

Once you arrive in the classroom, where you decide to sit is actually quite important. Many students do not give much thought to where they sit, but believe me, it will directly affect your learning. Certainly, I am not going to tell you exactly where you should and should not sit in the classroom. This is a matter of personal preference, so all I will say is that you should sit where you feel most comfortable and where you think you will learn the best.

Understand, however, that sitting in the same location for each class (i.e., in familiar surroundings) will improve your recall ability on test day. Also, realize that students are creatures of habit and will usually sit in the same general location or seat throughout the entire semester. Therefore, choose a location that will allow you to successfully engage in the class to facilitate your learning of the course material.

Engaging in the class can take various forms depending on the number of students in the course. It might involve answering questions posed by the instructor, participating in small group discussions, or simply listening attentively to lectures. Whatever form it takes, engaging in the class is vital to both your mastery of the course material and to your grade. In many courses, participation counts for 5 to 10 percent of your final grade. Yet one's ability to engage in the class is often personality driven.

Some students are very outgoing and can naturally interact with others or speak in public with ease. On the other hand, some students are quite shy, have difficulty interacting with others, and dread even the thought of speaking in public. Nonetheless, if you are a shy individual, I challenge you to start interacting more with others and to conquer your fear of public speaking.

In general, the vast majority of jobs and professions in our society involve working or directly interacting with others. This is why most colleges require students to work in small groups or complete group projects in many of their courses. It is their way of getting you ready for the "real world," where you will have to work with others on a daily basis in order to achieve a common goal. In short, you must strive to engage in each class session because it will help you master the course material, get a good grade, and of course, prepare you for life after college.

Engaging in the class and mastering the material also involves another important skill: taking good notes. I learned very early in my college career that taking notes was not just a mundane activity to pass the time during each class session. Conversely, I discovered that taking notes (and taking them well) was going to be crucial to my academic success in college, especially when it came time to study for tests.

Taking good notes is an acquired skill. Your notes should be organized, legible, and accessible. I mean, what is the purpose of taking notes if you cannot read them or easily locate specific information within them? The point I am trying to make is that if you put forth the effort to attend class, you should not just sit there and let your mind wander aimlessly while your instructor lectures. Listen attentively to lectures and diligently record notes, either by hand or with a voice recorder. The more times you process the course material, the better you will retain it. In addition, good notes will become a valuable study reference as you prepare for tests.

Finally, do not be afraid to ask questions when you need clarification. Students are often afraid to speak up in class when they do not understand something because they believe that others will mock them or think that they are stupid. However, chances are that if you do not understand something, then several of your fellow classmates feel the same way. So have the courage to speak up with your concerns as they arise.

Along the same lines, be sure to specifically inquire about test details. Your syllabus should have spelled out many of these details ahead of time, but quite often you can extract additional valuable information from your instructors by simply asking a few key questions. For instance, you might already know that your upcoming history test covers the first four chapters of the book and that it is multiple-choice. Nevertheless, try to narrow down some of the precise areas that you will need to focus on for the test.

Ask your instructors detailed questions pertaining to the test material and see how they respond. They might say, "I would focus on this" or "I would stay away from that," or they might not bite at all. Still, it never hurts to ask as it could pay huge dividends for you on test day. In my experience, I found that most instructors would usually give a few hints as long as somebody actually had the nerve to ask them. Again, it is always worth a shot. The worst that can happen is that they say nothing.

In this chapter, we have established that going to class is absolutely essential if you want to achieve academic success in college. Remember, you are paying good money for each and every class session on your schedule, so do not get in the habit of skipping classes. Besides, you want to get as much as possible out of each class session.

Accordingly, you should 1) be on time, 2) sit in a comfortable location, 3) engage in the class, 4) take good notes, and 5) ask questions when you need clarification. You should also be mindful of classroom distractions, particularly cell phones and chatty friends. Texting during class prevents you from truly engaging in the course material, and good friends do not always make good study partners.

In the next chapter, we will consider certain dynamics of the student-instructor relationship and how they can affect your grade. Most notably, we will discuss some tips and strategies that will assist you in establishing a good rapport with your instructors. This aspect of college academics is rarely considered, but I believe it to be of the utmost importance for achieving academic success in college.

Key Points:

- Skipping classes costs you big money and will put you behind in your studies.

- Arrive on time for each class session and sit where you feel comfortable.

- Actively engage in each class session to demonstrate participation and to facilitate mastery of course material.

- Listen attentively to lectures and take good notes, ensuring that they are organized, legible, and accessible.

- Ask questions during class if you need clarification about course material or test details.

- Avoid classroom distractions such as cell phones and chatty friends.

Chapter 5:
Establish a Good Rapport with Your Instructors

One aspect of college academics that is often overlooked by students is how vitally important it is to establish strong relationships with their instructors. No, I am not talking about socializing with your instructors outside of class or partaking in any other type of personal relationship, as these are both unprofessional and inappropriate. Conversely, I am referring to the significance of the student-instructor relationship and how it can affect your grade.

Throughout your college career, it will be crucial for you to establish a good rapport with your instructors, as this will positively affect your grades and provide you with a richer college experience. In this chapter, I will discuss a few tips and strategies that will help you establish sound relationships with your instructors. I will also provide valuable insights about the student-instructor relationship that I have acquired over the course of my college career in the hopes that you will be able to apply them to your own college experience.

It is well-known that professional educators are not usually rewarded monetarily for their endeavors. In fact, I firmly believe that educators at all levels in the United States are significantly underpaid for the enormous responsibility that they undertake, which is to educate the future workforce and leadership of this great nation. Even if someone dedicates his or her entire life to educating students, that person will certainly not become wealthy or retire rich. In reality, most educators consider themselves lucky if they even get tenure or a decent retirement pension.

As a result, it is pretty safe to assume that educators are not in it for the money. They choose to become lifelong educators because they love to teach and sincerely enjoy working with students. Their reward is the joy and satisfaction they receive from positively influencing the lives of their students and helping them succeed.

It is imperative to understand this reality when considering your education and your attitude toward college academics. It is also essential to recognize that college educators come from all walks of life. They possess expertise in various disciplines, and their approaches to teaching will be affected both by their professional training and by their own experiences as students. Thus, each of your instructors will be vastly different from the next, and you will have to learn and acclimate to each individual instructor's teaching style.

Regardless of their differences, there is one universal truth about all higher-level educators: they genuinely want you to succeed. Therefore, you can do yourself a big favor by interacting with your instructors on a regular basis: 1) participate in class, 2) ask questions, 3) talk with them before or after class, and 4) attend their office hours. Doing these things will demonstrate to your instructors that you are a serious student who is dedicated to learning and to getting the most out of your education.

Frequent interaction with your instructors will also assist you in getting to know each one's tendencies and will give you valuable insights as to what they expect in terms of classroom discussions, assignments, papers, and tests. Furthermore, it will help you better understand their values and beliefs, which will serve you well in the long-run. Although most instructors teach in an unbiased manner, some do let their personal convictions (e.g., political views, religious beliefs, and cultural values) influence their classroom conduct and, unfortunately, their grading.

Colleges and universities are places of enlightenment where you are encouraged to ask questions and to challenge the status quo in search of the truth. While this is certainly applicable to classroom discussions, tread lightly when it comes to directly assaulting your instructor's (or anyone else's) personal convictions, should they be revealed to you. Indeed, you are free to speak your mind during classroom discussions and to take stances in papers as you see fit, but your grade might be adversely affected if you challenge your instructor's personal convictions.

Instructors are only human, and it is very hard to be completely unbiased, especially when the topic of conversation or the content of a paper is particularly controversial or relates closely to their personal convictions. For instance, if you learned via classroom discussions that your instructor was a devout Christian, you might not want to write a paper on the nonexistence of God.

Now this is a little extreme, but I think you understand what I am trying to impress upon you: be careful about what you say during classroom discussions and the stances that you take in your papers. Do not get me wrong: I am not encouraging you to simply give the instructors what they want to hear, but you must consider the context of your situation before you proceed. If you do not, you might find yourself looking at your final grade and wondering why you received a C for the course instead of an A or a B. It is unfortunate, but this does happen from time to time in college academics and can happen to you if you are not careful.

Aside from direct contact with your instructors during class, interaction to establish a good rapport can also be achieved outside of the classroom. You will usually have the opportunity to speak with your instructors directly before or directly after class sessions. Most instructors arrive early to class and hang around for a few minutes afterward, which makes them a little more accessible to their students. If you find that there is not enough time to discuss the things on your mind before or after class, the easiest way to get your instructors' undivided attention is to attend their scheduled office hours.

All college and university instructors are required to hold dedicated "office hours" each week so that students have the opportunity to speak with them outside of the classroom. The actual number of office hours will vary depending on each instructor's course load and the size of the institution, but it usually ranges from four to eight hours per week.

Indeed, instructors at smaller colleges and universities are usually much more accessible than those at larger universities, where the *professors* are often preoccupied with research or with getting published. This is because larger universities pressure their professors to publish regularly in order to secure tenure and to gain or retain university prestige. Hence, at a larger university, you might only get a few minutes to speak with your instructors during their office hours, or you might be directed to speak with one of the teaching assistants (TA) instead. This can be somewhat of a barrier, but be persistent and make the best of what is available to you. TAs are often graduate students who have already taken the course and can therefore provide you with valuable insights and guidance.

On another note, some students are intimidated or afraid to speak with their instructors on an individual basis away from the classroom. Certainly, it can be a very intimidating experience when you enter an instructor's office and see all of his or her diplomas on the wall and the sea of books throughout the room. Still, you must understand that your instructors are there to help you and that they appreciate the extra effort that you make to interact with them outside of the classroom. Remember, they were college students once too and probably spent the better part of ten years in college at one level or another, so they know and appreciate what you are going through.

When you speak to an instructor one-on-one, use the time wisely and ask specific questions about course material and upcoming papers or tests. If you are undecided on a major, you can also use the time to inquire about potential fields of study, as many instructors are also academic advisors of some sort. Additionally, if you are interested in teaching, most instructors are more than happy to share their stories with you and tell you how to go about entering the world of professional academics.

No matter what you discuss while you are in your instructors' offices, the most important thing is that you are interacting with them and establishing a good rapport. Keep the conversation professional and focused on academics. Do not suck up and do not patronize them, as they will see right through it and know that you are just wasting their time. By ensuring that the conversation remains academically oriented, you will demonstrate to your instructor that you are a serious student who is focused on learning.

This type of interaction will promote a constructive, professional relationship that will enhance your college experience and positively influence your grades. It will also help your instructors remember who you are, as you will no longer be just another name on a long list of students. This can be particularly beneficial when they are grading papers and tests. They will see your name, put a face to it, and remember how committed you are to your education. Then, they will be more inclined to give you the benefit of the doubt if your grade for a paper or test is borderline.

In conclusion, establishing a good rapport with your instructors is a vitally important part of college academics. Doing so will provide you with a richer college experience and will positively affect your grades. You can achieve this by participating in class, asking questions, talking with your instructors before or after class, and attending their office hours.

Now that you are 1) in the right frame of mind, 2) organized, 3) going to class, and 4) establishing a good rapport with your instructors, you must set aside time to study and make the most of that study time. In the next chapter, we will discuss study tips as well as various strategies for maximizing your study time. So keep on reading. A good grade will be your reward!

Key Points:

- Professional educators love to teach and sincerely enjoy working with students.

- Each of your instructors will be vastly different from the next, and you will have to learn and acclimate to each individual instructor's teaching style.

- Interact with your instructors on a regular basis by participating in class, asking questions, talking with them before or after class, and attending their office hours.

- Do not be intimidated by or afraid to speak with your instructors. When you do, use the time wisely and ask specific questions related to the course material.

- Establishing a good rapport with your instructors will positively affect your grades and will provide you with a richer college experience.

CHAPTER 6:

Maximize Your Time

So it is Thursday night, and your friend calls you up to see if you want to go out. Between going to class and working part-time, it has been a stressful week, and you could certainly use a fun night out with your friends. However, you have a huge biology test tomorrow morning at eight o'clock and know that you are not as well prepared for it as you would like to be.

Although you have known about the test for weeks, you have procrastinated and have not studied much at all. Now, you will have to cram all night just to pull a passing grade. Consequently, there is no way that you could possibly go out tonight! As you sit down at your desk and begrudgingly open your biology book, anxiety begins to set in and you regret the fact that you waited until the last minute to study for the test.

College students find themselves in this situation all the time. Due to *procrastination* (i.e., putting it off), *distraction* (i.e., playing video games), *legitimate circumstances* (i.e., family emergency), or *sheer laziness*, a significant number of college students wait until the last minute to study for tests. This reality causes many unnecessary consequences, such as: 1) increased stress and anxiety, 2) poor concentration on test day from a lack of sleep the night before, and of course, 3) undesirable grades. The sad part about this is that it can all be prevented!

In the previous chapters, we discussed the importance of getting organized, going to class, and establishing a good rapport with your instructors. You could do all of these things well but still receive undesirable grades if you do not set aside time to study and make the most of that study time. Therefore, in this chapter, I will provide some tips and strategies that will help you maximize your study time. Keep in mind, however, that there are many different approaches to studying and that each individual student must find what works best for him or her. My goal is to simply expose you to the methodology that helped me prepare for tests and achieve a significant level of academic success throughout my college career.

College follows a cyclical and repetitious pattern over the course of the academic year. Depending on your school, the fall and spring semesters are usually about four months long and can therefore be broken down into thirds or fourths. Accordingly, assume that you will have a test in each course about once every four to five weeks.

Some instructors like to give one test per month and then a cumulative test during finals week, while other instructors will consider the fourth test to be the final test for the semester. Occasionally, you will just have a midterm test and a final test during the semester. Yet many instructors like to gauge their students' comprehension of the course material more frequently by giving monthly tests as the semester progresses.

As you recall, I discussed how to get organized in Chapter 3, "Live an Organized Life." Getting organized is crucial because it will help you utilize your time more effectively. This is absolutely true when it comes to studying for tests. Do not wait until the last minute to study! I can tell you from experience that pulling an "all-nighter" does not work. It only renders you exhausted, frustrated, and regretful that you did not put in the necessary study time prior to your test.

Your best approach is to set aside an hour or two each day to review your notes and begin preparing for any upcoming tests right away. I know this is a very difficult thing to do in college because of all the distractions (e.g., friends, computers, video games, athletics, fraternity/sorority events, parties, and so forth). In addition, your mom and dad will not be there to ride your case about studying or getting all of your homework done. In college, how, where, and when you study is entirely up to you.

Still, consider how this strategy adds up. If you study for two hours each day during the week, then you will have put in ten hours of study time by the end of the week. Breaking down the material throughout the week will help you retain the information better because your brain will not get overloaded, like it does when you cram. Besides, you cannot possibly study for ten hours straight the night before a test. Even if you pull an all-nighter, you will probably only get a few hours of quality study time. Then, you will be completely exhausted when you finally sit for the test.

Along with setting aside an hour or two every day to review your notes from each course, it is also very helpful to rewrite your class notes as well as any key passages from the reading material. This is a well-known and successful strategy for improving memory, but it is not commonly practiced because it can be quite time-consuming. Even so, I utilized this strategy frequently throughout my college career and found it to significantly improve both my short- and my long-term memory. The time I spent rewriting my notes and reading material paid off tremendously for me on test day, and it can do the same thing for you.

Rewriting your notes and reading material can be done in a variety of ways, but a common approach is to use note cards. Note cards, sometimes referred to as flash cards, are a great resource. As you break down the information and transcribe the most pertinent data onto note cards, you will simultaneously help yourself memorize the material and create a useful study aid in the process, which you can utilize later to review for tests.

Students often find it difficult to sift through page after page of the notes they took in the weeks leading up to a test. Thus, a way to simplify the study process is to highlight the most important themes, headings, terms, or definitions within your notes and then write them onto three-by-five note cards. You will find that it is much easier to focus on and memorize one card of information at a time than it is to trudge through page after page of notes. Dividing the material into manageable pieces helps simplify the study process, improve recall, and bolster performance on tests.

Last, it is utterly imperative that you find a good place to study. After all, you can spend hours and hours studying, but it will not be very productive if you are constantly surrounded by noises and distractions. So take it upon yourself to find a nice area or niche that is always available to you where you can go and put in quality study time. This might be a secluded part of the common area in your dorm facility or a quiet spot on the third floor of your school's library. Wherever it is, make sure that it is in a comfortable, convenient location and that you can study there without any distractions.

There are a few other things to consider in terms of maximizing study time. For instance, some people prefer to study in a group setting. This is a personal preference, and if it works for you, then by all means do so. Personally, I always retained information best when I could go over it by myself and at my own pace in a quiet, remote setting. Hence, I preferred to utilize an upper-level of the school library with minimal traffic. I found this setting to be the most productive for me in regard to studying and retaining information for tests.

Another aspect to think about is the possibility of setting yourself up to be distracted while you study. We obviously live in a technologically advanced society and rely heavily upon cell phones and computers for communication. Nonetheless, if you are trying to study but are constantly receiving phone calls, text messages, or alerts, then the quality of your study time will be significantly diminished. So try to resist the temptation to answer phone calls or to reply to text messages while you are studying unless it is absolutely necessary.

Similarly, many people claim that they need to have some background noise in order to study, so they listen to music or turn on the television. Once again, each person is different, so if it works for you, then do it. However, be wary of the potential for distraction as you mess with your MP3 player or glance over to the television to see what is happening.

Making time to study and utilizing that time wisely involves a lot more thought and planning than one might think. As we discussed in this chapter, there are many different approaches to studying, and each student will find what works best for him or her. I challenge you to set up and adhere to a strict study schedule. Doing so will significantly improve your comprehension of the course material, which will positively affect your grades.

Essentially, it is entirely up to you. You are in control of your own destiny and can make your own decisions about how, where, and when you study. Do not get me wrong: college is supposed to be "the best time of your life," and I want you to enjoy it. Nevertheless, you need to remember that you are in college for a purpose, and that purpose is to earn a degree. Believe it or not, a degree is not just handed to you after four or five years. You must invest a significant amount of time and effort to earn that degree. So by all means, be your own boss, but be aware of the consequences if you fail to make the right choices.

Now that we have outlined various study tips and ways that you can maximize your study time, let us take a more detailed look at test preparation. In the next chapter, we will discuss some of the psychology behind taking tests. We will also go over key test-taking strategies that will help you perform at your very best on test day. Finally, we will review some of the most common types of tests that you might encounter in college.

Key Points:

- Do not wait until the last minute to study for tests.

- Set aside an hour or two each day to review your notes and to begin preparing for any upcoming tests.

- Break down your study material into manageable pieces by rewriting the most pertinent data onto note cards.

- Find a place to study that is comfortable, convenient, always available, and free of distractions.

- Maximize the quality of your study time by avoiding unnecessary distractions such as cell phones, MP3 players, or computers.

CHAPTER 7:
Succeed Under Pressure—Taking Tests

Taking tests can be very stressful for many students and rightfully so, as test scores can account for one-third or even one-half of the entire grade for each course. Consequently, there is a great deal of pressure to perform well on test day. Yet quite often, students let their stress and anxiety get the best of them, which negatively affects their performance. So in this chapter, I want to highlight a few strategies that can help reduce your levels of stress and anxiety and allow you to reach your maximum potential on test day. I will also discuss some test-taking tips and a few basic details regarding the various types of tests you might encounter in college.

Some people are naturally good at taking tests, while others struggle with them significantly. Whether you believe it or not, it is something that you *can* improve upon with practice and repetition. In high school, I was relatively average at taking tests. Nevertheless, I became very good at it in college by developing a methodical approach to the process of test-taking, which ensured that I was always prepared for whatever I encountered on test day. Therefore, let us review some of the finer points of the system that I utilized throughout my college career to perform well on tests.

Reducing Test Anxiety

The primary key to this system is to address and control your test-taking anxiety. You must find a way to decrease your anxiety, both prior to and on test day. Doing so begins by employing a few of the concepts that we have already touched upon in this book: organization and dedicated study time.

In preparation for any test, you must organize and consolidate your study materials. Your instructor should have given you a general idea of what the test will cover. This information might have come from: 1) the syllabus, 2) points of emphasis during lectures, 3) classroom discussions, or 4) one-on-one dialogue with the instructor. Wherever the information comes from, you should be able to determine which areas to focus on for each test.

Once you have done this, skim through the reading material again and highlight any pertinent content that you might have missed the first time. You should also do the same thing with your notes from class and with any other supplemental study materials, such as handouts, audio recordings, note cards, and so forth. After you have consolidated all of your study materials, you can then begin committing the information to memory during dedicated study time.

There is no shortcut or easy way around it. If you want to do well on tests, you have to put in the study time. As we have already discussed, it is not good to wait until the last minute and pull an all-nighter the night before the test. Doing so will only set you up for failure: a fatigued mind cannot adequately absorb information, nor will it recall information with any degree of accuracy on test day.

Your best bet is to start preparing for the test a couple of weeks ahead of time. This allows you to break up the study material into manageable pieces and gradually commit the information to memory via repetition. It will take you a while to get through the information the first and second times, but with repetition comes speed. Before you know it, you will have memorized the vast majority of the information and will be able to recall it easily with little or no prompting from your study materials.

Putting in the study time and gaining command of your study materials prior to test day will significantly reduce your level of anxiety. Personally, I was always very, very nervous about tests in the weeks leading up to them. Yet the more time I put into studying the material, the less anxious I became, and by test day I had little or no anxiety whatsoever. I felt that I had done everything in my power to prepare and that actually taking the test was just a formality because I had such a good grasp of the material. My hope is that you can eventually get to this point so that on test day, you will perform at the highest level!

Test Day

Now that we have discussed a few strategies to help you decrease your anxiety prior to test day, let us talk about test day itself. Specifically, we will consider a few key tips in regard to preparing your mind and body for the test. Moreover, we will identify some ways to mitigate any underlying anxiety that might still exist on the big day.

As previously mentioned, it is essential that your mind be well-rested for test day. If you study the night before, set a reasonable stopping point so that you get a good night's sleep. This will help ensure that both your mind and your body are fully rested for the test. I also recommend that you eat a sensible breakfast, lunch, or dinner, depending on the time of your test. Your brain is a muscle and like all muscles, it needs fuel to perform at its best. Finally, wear comfortable clothing so that you do not feel any unnecessary bodily stress or pressure while taking the test.

In terms of mitigating any underlying anxiety that might still exist on test day, this will really depend on each individual person. Some students prefer to exercise right before taking tests to help reduce stress and release valuable endorphins, while others prefer to look over their notes one last time. I found the latter to be helpful.

Although I always felt fully prepared prior to test day, I squashed any remnants of anxiety by processing the material one last time on test day right before the test. I felt that processing the material once again kept the information fresh in my mind and helped me stay focused. Whatever you decide to do on test day to ease your anxiety, make sure that it is something that will help you perform well on the test itself. It might take some time to figure out what works for you, but once you find the best course of action, work it into your routine before each test thereafter.

Types of Tests

Some college success books dedicate lengthy chapters on how to take certain types of tests (see *FOCUS on College Success* by Constance Staley).[4] Therefore, I am not going to go over every single detail of each type of test that you might encounter in college. Conversely, I am simply going to review a few basic tactics and considerations that helped me do well on the various types of tests that I encountered in college.

Generally speaking, you will have three main types of tests in college: 1) multiple-choice, 2) short-answer/fill-in-the-blank, and 3) essay. Hands down, the most common of these is the multiple-choice test. In many cases, the test will consist solely of multiple-choice questions. Nevertheless, you must also be prepared for a combination of multiple-choice, short-answer, and essay questions.

No matter what type of test you are taking, it is essential to read each question carefully. Often, students answer questions incorrectly because they either read through them too quickly or do not understand what the questions are actually asking. So read each question closely and reread those that do not make sense to you the first time.

Multiple-Choice Tests

Let us first consider multiple-choice tests. After you have read and understood exactly what the question is asking, see if you can think of the correct answer before looking at any of the possible choices. Sometimes, looking at the choices too soon can confuse you or convince you that another answer makes more sense.

Obviously, if you know the correct answer, circle it and move on to the next question. However, if you do not have the absolute best answer identified in your mind, you should use the process of elimination to make an "educated guess." Process of elimination will help you identify those answers that fall short or those that simply do not make sense. In doing so, you should be able to leave yourself with two possible choices. Then, you have a fifty-fifty chance of selecting the correct answer.

When it comes to multiple-choice tests, a common misconception is that you should just guess C if you do not know the correct answer. This is completely absurd! Guessing C on all the questions that you do not know will not serve you well. Again, when you do not know the absolute correct answer to a particular question, use the process of elimination to narrow down the choices and make an educated guess.

Furthermore, on multiple-choice tests, do not go back and change your answers! Always go with your gut feeling. Your first inclination is usually the correct one, and going back to change answers will only get you into trouble. I fought this habit throughout my college career; when I went back and changed answers, I almost always got them wrong.

Finally, if you did not study much and are not quite prepared for the multiple-choice test, read through and answer the questions that you *do* know first. Then, go back later and work on the questions that you do not know. This will ensure that you make it through all of the test questions and answer the ones that you know as opposed to struggling through question after question that you do not. In addition, some questions later in the test might provide you with clues to the correct answers in the previous questions that you did not know.

Short-Answer/Fill-in-the-Blank Tests

Once again, multiple-choice tests are the most prevalent type of test in college. Tests that have exclusively short-answer/fill-in-the-blank questions are quite rare. These types of questions are usually a component of either a multiple-choice or an essay test. Regardless, with short-answer/fill-in-the-blank questions, you either know the answer or you do not. There is really no way around it. Your best bet is to brainstorm and just do the best you can. Whatever the case, try not to leave any of the answers completely blank. Even if you do not know the correct answer, you might still receive partial credit if you make an effort or come close.

Essay Tests

Essay tests are given most frequently in the social science and humanities courses (e.g., history, philosophy, sociology, religion, and so forth). In order to successfully answer an essay question, you need to clearly articulate your thoughts. A good rule of thumb is to rewrite the question in the introduction of your answer. For instance, if the essay question asks, "What were the causes of the American Revolution, and how did those causes influence rebellion in other countries?" you should begin your answer by stating: "There were many factors that caused the American Revolution and influenced rebellion in other countries ..."

After completing your introduction, you should provide at least three or four pieces of supporting information by citing specific authors or research that lends support and credibility to your answer. Once you have provided sufficient supporting evidence, you should end your response with a conclusion. Again, this involves restating the question: "In conclusion, there were many factors that caused the American Revolution and influenced rebellion in other countries ..."

Successfully answering an essay question is a lot like writing a good paper, which we will discuss in greater detail in the next chapter. In the meantime, remember to convey complete thoughts with proper spelling, syntax, and punctuation when answering essay test questions.

True/False Tests

Now a word on some of the less common types of tests that you might encounter in college: 1) true/false, 2) open-book, and 3) take-home tests. Much like short-answer questions, true/false questions will probably not constitute the entire test but will rather be a component of a larger test. Here, I must reiterate the fact that you need to read each question carefully. True/false questions can be quite tricky, and oftentimes, the adverbs used within the questions will dictate whether the answer is true or false. Therefore, pay close attention to the language of each question, particularly the use of *negatives* (e.g., no, not, cannot); *qualifiers* (e.g., sometimes, often, generally); and *absolutes* (e.g., always, never, every). These can make true/false questions very confusing.

Open-Book Tests

Open-book tests administered within the classroom are very, very rare in college. Still, if you do have an open-book test, understand that the questions are usually much more difficult than those on any other type of classroom test. Obviously, this is due to the very fact that you get to use your textbooks, notes, and other resources to answer the questions.

Open-book tests are challenging because the questions are often pulled from rather obscure locations within the textbook or are developed directly from the instructor's lecture material. Hence, you can spend a great deal of time looking for just one answer, especially if you are not familiar with the textbook readings or did not take good lecture notes during each class session.

Accordingly, you must use your time wisely. If you are taking a sixty-question test and only have two hours to complete it, do not spend five minutes looking for the answer to just one question. At that rate, it would take you five hours to finish the test! Manage your allotted time carefully and, as with any other type of test, answer the questions that you know first and then go back to the ones you do not.

Take-Home Tests

Last but not least, let us talk briefly about take-home tests. These also are very uncommon in college. When they do occur, though, they can be both a blessing and a curse. Some people love take-home tests because they do not experience the anxiety leading up to test day. However, take-home tests are usually composed of very detailed short-answer and essay questions. Accordingly, they can be quite difficult and time-consuming.

As previously established, open-book tests are made to be more difficult because you get to use your textbooks and notes. Along the same lines, instructors expect a higher quality of work on take-home tests because you have more time and better resources to formulate your responses. So understand that in order to do well on take-home tests, you will have to invest just as much, if not more, time as you would have in preparation for a traditional test within the classroom.

On another note, keep in mind that the goal of test-taking is not to finish as soon as possible, as one does not earn extra points for finishing first. It always amazed me when some of my peers would complete a sixty-minute test in twenty minutes. Perhaps they just knew the information that well (or not at all) and sailed right through all of the questions. Whether they knew the information or not, I bet they missed at least two or three questions simply because they read through the test too fast. So what should you do with extra time as it relates to any test?

Once more, use your time judiciously. If you finish a test early, skim through it a second time to make sure that you did not skip a question or accidentally circle a wrong answer because you went too quickly. Also, if it is a Scantron test, use any extra time to make sure that you filled in the correct bubbles on your Scantron sheet. After all, you spent a significant amount of time studying and preparing for your test, so the last thing that you want to do is lose points because you went too fast or made clerical errors.

Last, if you completely blew off studying and are not prepared for a test, do not resort to cheating. Cheating is unacceptable at any level of academics, and if you are caught, you will pay a hefty price. The best thing that can happen to you if you are caught cheating is to receive an F or a zero for that particular test. Yet you could also be dismissed from the course or expelled from the school altogether. Whatever the case, it is just not worth it. Do your own work, learn from your mistakes, and try to prepare better for the next test. You might only get a C or a D on a particular test if you are not prepared, but that is better than any of the other possible outcomes if you are caught cheating.

In this chapter, we highlighted a few strategies to help you reduce your levels of stress and anxiety so that you can reach your maximum potential on test day. We also discussed some test-taking tips and a few basic details regarding the various types of tests that you might encounter in college. Remember, it is important that you develop a reliable system that works for you as you prepare for test day. Once it arrives, take a deep breath and relax. If you have utilized some of the aforementioned tips and strategies to prepare for the test, then you should have no problem earning a top grade!

Key Points:

- You can become a great test-taker through preparation, practice, and repetition.

- Reduce your test-taking anxiety by organizing your study materials and committing the information to memory during dedicated study time.

- The more prepared you are for a test, the less anxious you will be prior to and on test day.

- Ensure that your mind and body are fully rested for test day, and try to practice the same routine before each test.

- Read each test question carefully so that you do not miss something.

- Manage your time wisely: answer the questions that you know first and then go back to the ones that you do not know later.

- Use the process of elimination to make an educated guess on the questions that you do not know.

- Once you have completed the test, review it to make sure that you did not make any clerical errors. However, do not go back and change your answers.

CHAPTER 8

Write Great Papers

Without question, writing is an art form. Very few people are naturally gifted writers who can just sit down and produce excellent work at a young age. On the contrary, writing is an acquired skill that must be meticulously developed and continuously improved upon over the course of one's life. The process of becoming a proficient writer begins in childhood when one enters school and continues well into college.

Indeed, writing is often a very tedious endeavor, but it gets easier with time and repetition. Believe me, you will notice a substantial increase in the quality of your writing as you complete each year of college. Accordingly, in this chapter, I would like to help you become a better writer by reviewing some specific tips, tools, and strategies for writing papers that served me well throughout my college education.

Writing Formats

I am not going to articulate to you the finer points of the many different writing formats used in college. After all, depending on the course you are taking and your instructor, you might have to be well versed in more than one of them. For instance, if you are taking an English course, you will probably be required to write in the Modern Language Association (MLA) format. Conversely, if you are taking a psychology, nursing, or any other science course, you will be required to write in the American Psychological Association (APA) or American Medical Association (AMA) format. Furthermore, most scholarly history courses embrace the Chicago/Turabian format.

As a result, it is clear that a detailed explanation of each of these individual writing formats would consume the vast majority of this book. In fact, nearly every writing format has its own publication manual that you can either check out at the campus library or purchase yourself. I recommend purchasing the manual that you will use most often because it will be a tremendous asset to you as you write papers. For instance, if you are a history major, you should get a copy of *A Manual for Writers of Research Papers, Theses, and Dissertations* by Kate L. Turabian.[5]

To ensure that you turn in a quality and complete paper, take the extra time to format your paper correctly. The importance of proper formatting cannot be overstated, as it can account for anywhere from 5 to 20 percent of the final grade of a paper. In lieu of providing complete outlines of each of the different writing formats, let us focus on the writing process instead.

The Writing Process

When starting any paper, the first thing you should do is carefully read over the guidelines for it. At minimum, most instructors should provide you with the following guidance: 1) the proposed topic, 2) the desired length, 3) the required format, 4) the grading details, and 5) the due date. You need to have a firm grasp of these points before beginning any paper composition.

The second step is to develop and set a timeline for yourself. Smaller papers are often due in a week or two, but larger research papers are usually assigned at the beginning of the course and are not due for several weeks. Therefore, if you are disciplined, you should always have ample time to complete any paper. The key to success is organization and planning, both of which can be achieved by establishing goals and deadlines for completing each portion of the paper.

For example, let us say that you have a five- to seven-page research paper due in four weeks. This might seem overwhelming if you do not consider yourself to be good at writing papers, especially given the demands of your other courses. Nevertheless, take it one step at a time and set several little goals and deadlines. Breaking up the workload of the paper will do two things: it will give you a plan of attack to get the paper done on time, and it will reduce your anxiety. As you complete each goal or deadline, you will feel a sense of accomplishment and will know that you are firmly in control of the project. Now, back to our example.

Four weeks may seem like a lot of time, and it is easy to procrastinate until the last minute to begin your paper. However, procrastinating will only cause you unnecessary stress and will set you up for failure. Most important, the finished product will be less than adequate, which will result in a poor grade. Hence, during the first week, your goal might be to complete the outline for your research paper.

Introduction of the Paper

A quality paper is based on an outline that consists of three essential components: the introduction, the body, and the conclusion. The introduction should briefly identify the topic of the paper, provide a few intriguing facts about the subject to set up the discussion, and outline the major points that you are attempting to make. Composing a solid introduction is key, as it will set the tone for your entire paper and will garner interest from the reader (i.e., your instructor). The following is an example of a good introduction from an environmental paper that I wrote in college:

In today's fast-paced and modern world, American families rarely prepare and eat all of their meals at home. In fact, it is estimated that more than half of the average American household food budget is spent on meals outside the home.[6] So where do most Americans get their sustenance?

The reality is that a large portion of Americans eat out, particularly at fast-food restaurants. This trend has drastically contributed to the obesity epidemic in America. Thus, the focus of this environmental paper is to identify the correlation between eating out at fast-food restaurants and obesity. Specifically, the research will demonstrate that the sheer number of fast-food restaurants in America is one of the main contributors to the obesity crisis in this country.

Body of the Paper

After completing the introduction, you will move on to the meat of the paper: the body. It contains all of the important details related to your topic, such as the background information, pertinent facts, and supporting research. If you are writing a position or research paper, it will also include the data that supports your stance on the topic or lends credibility to your research hypothesis. In most research papers, you will be required to take a stance on a particular topic and then support it with relevant and contemporary research.

The body should make up the bulk of any paper. Let us use our five- to seven-page research paper example. In this case, the introduction should be about one page, the body should be about five pages, and the conclusion should be about one page. The exact breakdown of each element will depend on you, but this is generally a good pattern to follow. By no means should either the introduction or the conclusion be longer than the body of your paper. If they are, then you did not provide enough background information, facts, or research to support your topic.

Conclusion of the Paper

Once you have completed the body, you need to develop a strong conclusion. If you were a lawyer, this would be your closing argument. It is the last part of the paper that your instructor is going to read, so you want it to be clear, crisp, and concise. The conclusion should restate the topic and briefly summarize the main point(s) you have made to support your position or research hypothesis. The following is an example of a good conclusion from the same environmental paper:

Fast-food restaurants are very prevalent in America and are clearly a major contributor to the national obesity epidemic in this country. This is a significantly important public health issue because in numerous cities, the vast number of fast-food restaurants have created toxic environments that offer few choices for healthy nutritional consumption. This is a major environmental hazard for the American population as a whole. Therefore, health policy at the municipal level should seek to regulate the number of fast-food restaurants that can open for business in any one geographical area, especially in areas where obesity is already endemic.

Citing Resources/Plagiarism

While you are working on each component of the paper, it is very important that you properly cite any resources or research that you use to compose your paper. Failure to do so is called **plagiarism**, which is the unlawful copying of another individual's work and then presenting it as your own.[7] Schools and instructors at every level are very strict on plagiarism, and rightfully so. In fact, many schools now use software programs to monitor for it. Essentially, they can scan your paper and compare it with a database that contains millions of pages of documents. The software program then highlights any areas that might be considered plagiarism and prints out a report indicating how much of the paper is plagiarized.

If you are caught plagiarizing, you will probably receive an F or a zero on the paper. You could also be dismissed from the course entirely. In more severe or repetitive cases of plagiarism, you could even be expelled from the school. Sure, it is much easier and less time-consuming to copy someone else's work, but plagiarism is simply unacceptable at any level, so just do not do it. Much like cheating on a test, it is not worth ending your college career by engaging in plagiarism. Do your own work and cite any resources or research that you use accordingly.

Okay, so how do you go about citing the resources and research that you use when writing papers? Again, it will depend on which writing format your paper calls for. Each writing format has a very different way of citing resources and research. It could involve the use of footnotes or endnotes and a corresponding bibliography, works cited, or reference page. Once more, I highly recommend that you refer to the publication manual of the particular writing format that your paper requires. Not only will it help you format your paper correctly, it will specifically outline how to cite each and every type of resource that you used to compose your paper.

Paper Timeline/Proofreading

Now, let us get back to the timeline for writing your paper. Using our example of a five- to seven-page research paper that is due in four weeks, I recommended that you use the first week to develop your outline. Once this is done, you should utilize the second week to gather resources and research that can be used to compose your paper. During the third week, you should start writing the bulk of the paper and complete a rough draft. Finally, the last week should be used for proofreading, rewriting, and completing your final draft.

Once you have completed your final draft, you should have somebody else proofread it for spelling, grammar, syntax, formatting, and logical flow of ideas. I found this to be very helpful because no matter how many times I would proofread my work, I always seemed to miss a few things. That is because your mind tends to read over a document the same way each time, thus allowing for mistakes to be missed. In other words, your mind knows what you are trying to say and might not realize that you actually used an incorrect word or switched the order of two words here or there. That is why having another person proofread your paper is so beneficial. He or she will read the document for what it actually says and will likely not read over any mistakes that you made.

Along the same lines, do not rely solely on computer programs to fix your spelling, grammar, syntax, or formatting mistakes. For instance, the words *to, two,* and *too* all have very different meanings, yet when placed in the context of a sentence, a computer program might not recognize that you used one of these words incorrectly. Two other words that many computer programs fail to identify when used erroneously are *there* and *their.* Once again, have another person proofread your paper, as there are numerous examples of these sorts of mistakes and someone else will more than likely pick up on them.

Help Is Available

Finally, there are a couple of other things to consider when writing papers. First, almost all schools offer writing labs or writing workshops to assist students in writing papers (see Chapter 11, "If All Else Fails," for more details). This is particularly helpful if you are struggling with the writing process or want to have your paper proofread by somebody who is a very proficient writer. Second, some instructors will allow you to bring in a rough draft of your paper and will briefly review it to see if you are on the right track. In any case, use your time and campus resources wisely when writing papers.

In this chapter, we went over some specific tips, tools, and strategies for writing papers that served me well throughout my college education. By no means was this a complete step-by-step guide on how to write within the confines of each of the different writing formats. Rather, it was more of a basic overview to help you begin the process of writing great papers. Once more, writing is a skill that can be honed with time, practice, and repetition. I am confident that you will become a proficient writer as your college career progresses and that the quality of your papers will be reflected in the grades that you receive!

In the next chapter, we will discuss another vital component of your academic experience in college: group projects.

Key Points:

- Writing is an acquired skill that must be meticulously developed and continuously improved upon. Yet it gets easier with time and repetition.

- Determine which writing format is required for each of your papers and strictly adhere to that format's protocols.

- In order to get your paper done on time, read the guidelines carefully and then develop a timeline by which to complete each portion of the paper.

- A quality paper consists of three essential components: the introduction, the body, and the conclusion.

- Cite all of your references diligently, and do not plagiarize another person's work.

- Do not rely solely on computer programs: have somebody else proofread your paper to locate errors in spelling, grammar, syntax, and formatting.

CHAPTER 9

Take Charge of Group Projects

G roup projects can be a very challenging aspect of your academic experience in college. Your school's philosophy will determine how much experience you will have working in group projects. For instance, prior to attending Grand View University, I attended a college for one year that mandated that each course, no matter the subject, have a group project as part of the student's overall grade. This was both enlightening and infuriating at the same time!

Why Group Projects?

It is no secret: the purpose of group projects in college is to help students become comfortable working and interacting with others in order to reach a common goal. Basically, you are supposed to learn how to "play nicely" with others prior to entering the workforce because once you graduate and get a job, you will have to interact and cooperate with other people on a daily basis.

Working with others—such as your boss, coworkers, employees, business associates, patrons, clients, or patients—will be required in just about any job you ever have in life. Unless you work from home or live in a bubble, you will not be able to avoid human interaction. Now that we understand the logic behind group projects, let us take a closer look at some of their dynamics and how you can set yourself up for success.

In addition to attendance, participation, papers, and tests, group projects will usually account for some portion of your final grade in most courses, typically anywhere from 10 to 25 percent of the overall grade. Hence, group projects are not something that should be taken lightly.

The Downside of Group Projects

To be completely honest, I was never very fond of group projects because I often found myself doing most of the work. In my experience, this was because in nearly every group project, approximately one-third of the group members were of little or no assistance to the overall project. This is a pretty common theme when it comes to group projects, and it occurs for a variety of reasons. Primarily, it is because one-third of the individuals are lazy, do not produce quality work, or simply do not care. Whatever the case, just realize that on average, one-third of the individuals in your group will be of no value to the project.

This reality is very, very frustrating for those students who want to do well on the project. What usually happens is that you have to either carry the extra workload for the individuals who are not contributing or call them out on their lack of effort. Either approach creates tension among the group members and can lead to open conflict.

Understand that you will rarely be in a group where everyone shares the workload equally and submits quality work for the overall project. Knowing this in advance will help you get through each group project experience. Realize that if you are like me and want to earn that top grade, you will be putting in a great deal of work. More often than not, you will be the one responsible for typing up the paper, developing the PowerPoint presentation, or actually presenting the project to the class.

If a certain individual in your group is not pulling his or her weight, you can choose from a few courses of action. First and foremost, I would recommend that you talk to that individual and simply ask why he or she is not contributing to the project. If this does not help remedy the situation, you could speak to the TA or to the instructor and inform them that the individual in question is not actively participating in the project. If all else fails, you can call attention to that individual's lack of contribution in his or her peer evaluation.

Most instructors will ask you to rate each of your fellow group members on their participation and contribution to the project. This rating will usually account for 5 to 15 percent of each individual's total grade for the project. So you might receive an A on the project because of your strong peer evaluations, and another member of your group might receive a B because he or she failed to put forth much effort.

Now that we have discussed some of the negative aspects of group projects, let us consider some of the ways that they can be a positive experience. Specifically, we will look at how you can contribute and be a productive member of the group.

The Upside of Group Projects

One positive aspect of group projects is that you get to meet and work with new people. In other words, you get to "network," which is a crucial aspect of both the college experience and the professional working environment. Knowing a variety of people in diverse positions and from all walks of life will help you easily relate to others on multiple levels.

This will serve you well because as you get to know more and more people, you will be able to demonstrate to them your worth as a member of the group. You will be able to showcase your skills as a leader, a follower, and a team player. Over time, you will begin to develop a reputation for yourself, and people will know exactly what you are capable of doing, both good and bad.

So as you meet the people in your group for the first time, you will want to make a good first impression. One of the ways you can do this is by volunteering to take ownership of a certain aspect of the project. After all, in a group setting, everybody likes it when somebody else steps up to the plate. Thus, you might volunteer to serve as the group leader or the assistant group leader, if those positions are not already assigned by the instructor. On the other hand, if you are more of a shy individual, you do not necessarily have to volunteer for a leadership position. However, do not be too bashful about volunteering your services in other areas.

Volunteering to take on a specific area of the project will demonstrate to the other group members that you genuinely want to contribute and are serious about the outcome of the project. It will also help break the ice if you do not really know any of the other group members. Last, it will help ensure that the project responsibilities are divided equally and shared by all of the group members.

During the first group meeting, the members should collectively review the project requirements, begin to divide the responsibilities, discuss group expectations, and develop a timeline by which to have certain portions of the project completed. You should also set a schedule of future meeting times and locations to work on the project as a group.

Identify Strengths and Weaknesses

As you work on the project and get to know your fellow group members better, you will begin to identify each individual's strengths and weaknesses. Use this to your advantage, and as a group, tailor responsibilities accordingly. For example, if one of the group members is a whiz at PowerPoint, it would make sense for that person to develop and fine-tune the presentation media. Similarly, if one of the group members articulates very well and does not mind speaking in front of others, perhaps he or she should present the project in class.

The bottom line is that everyone is good at something. The trick is to figure out who is good at what and use it to benefit the group as a whole. Properly assigning tasks and responsibilities will help the project run smoothly and will positively influence the outcome.

Completing the Work

In terms of meeting times and locations, it is imperative that these are convenient for all group members. If not, it might be difficult to get everyone together to work on the project. Try to select reasonable times to meet. I found that most of my group meetings occurred on Sunday or Monday evenings. Nevertheless, each group must determine what works best for its members.

As a group member, make sure that you are always on time for the group meetings. Your peers have busy schedules, and the last thing that they want to do is sit around and wait for you to show up. Being late for meetings is very disrespectful to them and wastes valuable time. Furthermore, come to the meetings well prepared. Make sure that you have your individual work completed and ready to show to the group. By being punctual and productive, you will further demonstrate to the other group members that you are serious about the outcome of the project. This will give you credibility as a group member and will facilitate professional working relationships with your peers.

As for writing the group paper, developing the presentation materials, and presenting the project, you should strive to divide the workload equally. Depending on the size of your group, you should assign each of these tasks to different people. In other words, the person presenting the project should not also have to develop all of the presentation materials. By assigning these tasks to different people, you allow each individual to focus on his or her one specific task, which will enhance the overall quality of the project. Also, if you have enough people, perhaps you can even assign two individuals to each main task.

Checks and Balances

Once each main task is complete, you should have each group member review the work in order to create a system of checks and balances. For instance, if you were responsible for writing the group paper, print copies of the completed paper and ask the other group members to critique it. Perhaps you forgot to include a key piece of information or did not format the paper correctly. The other group members will surely recognize these inconsistencies and will offer feedback to enhance the overall quality of the final product.

Finally, have the presenters practice rehearsing the presentation in front of the group. Provide constructive criticism about the flow of the presentation, their ability to maintain eye contact with the audience, and so forth. Furthermore, ask the presenters a few questions so that they are prepared to answer inquiries from the class or the instructor on presentation day.

Presentation Day

Once presentation day arrives, be sure to get to class early enough to meet with your group one more time to go over any last-minute details. If you are one of the presenters, relax and trust in your preparation. If you are not, be as supportive as possible to those who are presenting. Help them set up the presentation media and distribute any handouts. After the presentation is over, provide positive reinforcement to the presenters and to the other group members as well.

Once the project is totally completed, you will feel a tremendous sense of relief. In due time, you will also find out what grade you received. Hopefully, it will be the grade that you wanted. If not, take note of things that went wrong with this project so you can improve for the next one. Trust me: you will have plenty of opportunities to work out the kinks!

In conclusion, group projects can be both enlightening and infuriating at the same time. The opportunity to meet and network with new people is very valuable. However, if your fellow group members are not quite up to par, do not let frustration get the best of you. Be patient and work through any issues in a professional manner. Also, remember to volunteer your talents and to be a team player at all times. If you understand the dynamics of group projects and the ways that you can positively contribute, I am confident that you will earn that top grade!

Key Points:

- Group projects help students learn how to work with others in order to achieve a common goal.

- Group projects are a great way to meet new people and to network with peers.

- First impressions are key: volunteer your services to the group to demonstrate that you are a team player and that you are motivated to succeed.

- Take charge of group projects: identify each individual's strengths and weaknesses, then tailor responsibilities accordingly.

- Divide the workload evenly and review one another's work to ensure quality.

- On average, one-third of the individuals in your group will be of little or no value to the overall project, so be prepared to pick up the extra slack.

CHAPTER 10:
Understand Online Courses

Online courses are becoming more and more prevalent in college academics today. Some colleges are completely online-based, whereas others offer both traditional classroom courses and online courses. At some point in your college career, you will probably find yourself enrolled in an online course. Therefore, it is important that you understand how online courses work and what is expected of you as a student. In this chapter, I will discuss the various aspects of online courses and some of the things that you can do to set yourself up for success. We will also talk about online discussion forums and how you should conduct yourself in them.

Background

The demand for increased accessibility to higher education in this country has fueled a surge in distance learning over the past ten years. In the 2006–2007 school year, there were approximately 11,200 college-level programs designed to be completed entirely through distance education. During this same time period, there were an estimated 12.2 million registrations in distance learning courses, of which nearly 77 percent were in online courses.[8] These are the most current statistics available from the US Department of Education, so it is safe to assume that they have increased significantly since.

Currently, there are more online colleges than ever before offering everything from associate's to doctoral degrees. In fact, even some of the most established "brick and mortar" schools are starting to offer online courses as an adjunct to their traditional classroom courses. Doing so enhances enrollment, provides more options for students, and generates more revenue for the schools.

Besides simply increasing accessibility to higher education, however, online courses are becoming more popular with students because of sheer convenience. Online courses offer a tremendous amount of flexibility that is not typically available in the traditional classroom setting. Essentially, all that a student needs to participate in an online course is a reliable computer and Internet access. The prospect of attending classes from home is more appealing because students do not have to waste time commuting or have to pay for parking. In short, time is money, and many students feel that their time is better spent by taking online courses. This is especially true for students who work full- or part-time or have to move frequently because of their jobs.

What It Takes to Succeed

Just like in traditional classroom courses, you must be well-organized, disciplined, and motivated in order to succeed in online courses. You will still have assignments and deadlines, and failing to complete the course requirements will negatively affect your grade. Nevertheless, two key differences between online courses and traditional classroom courses are how you demonstrate participation and how you submit your work.

As with any course, you should receive a syllabus from your instructor that outlines the course schedule and all of the course requirements. In most online courses, you will still have required readings, papers, and tests. Depending on your instructor, you might even have to complete a group project. Nonetheless, a chief distinction of an online course is how you demonstrate to your instructor that you are fully engaged in the course. This is typically done by submitting online "message posts."

Message Posts

Although some online courses have interactive lectures where students can respond directly to their instructors via audio/video feeds, this is not always the case. Accordingly, the instructors must come up with alternative methods to promote participation, facilitate discussion, and gauge their students' comprehension of the course material. In order to do this, most instructors will pose a question about the lecture material or about one of the readings in an online message forum. Each student is then required to submit a thoughtful response to that question or respond to another student's post.

The number of posts that you will be required to make each week will vary, but there are several things to consider when posting your thoughts. First and foremost, both your instructor and your fellow classmates will see everything that you post. Hence, make certain that your posts are clearly articulated and are of substance. For instance, do not simply reply to another student's post by saying, "I agree." This reflects minimal effort on your part, and your instructor will probably not give you any points for it. Take a little extra time and post thought-provoking responses that are supported by the readings, research, or lecture material. A three- to five-sentence post is ideal. Be certain to cite any references that you use, and do not add extra fluff just to lengthen the post.

As for the content of your posts, you must be very careful about what you say and how it comes across. The same etiquette that we discussed earlier in regard to classroom conduct applies to online courses and message posts as well. Keep your comments professional at all times, and do not post anything that could be considered controversial. Remember, it is hard to decipher emotion and points of emphasis in typed text. You might be trying to say one thing, but it could be misinterpreted or taken completely out of context. In turn, this could negatively affect your participation grade and could alienate you from your instructor or classmates. So once again, submit academically oriented posts in a timely and respectful manner to ensure that you receive maximum points for participation.

Taking Tests in Online Courses

In terms of completing required readings, writing papers, and taking tests, you will not notice much of a difference in online courses as compared to traditional classroom courses. The only minor disparity relates to test-taking. Obviously, you will be required to take tests using electronic means instead of paper and pencil. There will usually be a time limit placed on each test, and it will appear on your computer screen in the form of a digital countdown. Pay close attention to the countdown because once the time expires, the test is automatically submitted. Conversely, when you run out of time in a traditional classroom course, you can sometimes get a few extra minutes, depending on the situation or your instructor.

Some online courses will not allow you to take tests electronically from home. Occasionally, you might have to go to a testing center or to a local community college to have the test proctored. In this case, the test is administered by a trained professional who closely monitors you to ensure that the integrity of the test is maintained. Here, you will take the test either electronically or with paper and pencil.

Group Projects in Online Courses

Group projects, on the other hand, are conducted somewhat differently in online courses. Due to the fact that you typically cannot meet with the other group members in person, getting everyone on the same page can often be very difficult. Furthermore, the logistical aspect of gathering research and sharing documents can be rather tedious. Over time, your e-mail inbox will be flooded with correspondence from the other group members and, at one point or another, somebody will have to piece all of the information together into one final product.

In any case, communication is absolutely essential when working on group projects in online courses. Despite being geographically separated, you must coordinate to "meet" (i.e., get on the computer) at the same time and devise effective means to share the workload. It can be tricky to coordinate meeting times, especially if some of the other group members live in different time zones.

In the end, some group members will be more reliable than others, and essentially, many of the same dynamics that we discussed in Chapter 9, "Take Charge of Group Projects," will still apply. If you are having trouble with a group member, try to contact him or her and remedy the situation. Perhaps there is an issue with his or her computer or Internet connectivity. If that is the case, it is usually understandable. If, however, you find out that the person is blatantly ignoring e-mails or message posts, then you should probably inform your instructor.

In addition, if for some reason you cannot reach a group member via e-mail or messaging, do not always assume that you will be able to call him or her. Some students are very reluctant to give out their phone numbers and prefer to only communicate electronically. In that situation, contact your instructor because he or she may have more information as to why the student in question has not responded to your e-mails or message posts.

Submitting Assignments

When it comes to submitting assignments, such as papers or projects, it is imperative that you leave yourself some time in case you experience any glitches during the submission process. For example, do not wait until two minutes before the deadline to start the process of submitting an assignment. Technology is a wonderful thing, but it is not perfect and several glitches could occur during the process: 1) your computer could freeze up, 2) you could temporarily lose Internet connectivity, 3) the host server could go down, or 4) it could simply take longer than you expected to upload and send the attachment. Whatever the case, be sure to plan accordingly and allow yourself plenty of time to meet all required submission deadlines.

When submitting assignments or message posts, you also need to be conscious of any time zone differences. For instance, if you are in a time zone that uses Pacific Standard Time but your college is located in a time zone that uses Eastern Standard Time, understand that there is a three-hour time disparity and that you will need to plan accordingly when submitting work. Most online course home pages have a clock that is used as the standard timekeeper for all course-related deadlines. The easiest way to ensure that you do not miss a deadline is to calculate any time zone difference at the beginning of the course and be mindful of it for the duration.

Software Programs

Colleges use a variety of software programs to service and administer online courses. Some purchase rights to use existing software, such as Blackboard, whereas other colleges develop and maintain their own software. At any rate, most software programs used for online courses provide many of the same features. It is important for you to know about some of these features and how to use them properly while you are taking any online course. In fact, you might even use programs like Blackboard in some of your traditional classroom courses.

Undoubtedly, one of the standard features in any program is the message forum, which is sometimes referred to as a message board. This feature is very simple to use. All you have to do is type a message into the dialogue box and then click Submit. Just realize that each topic will be identified by its own category or "thread" and that all message posts will be stamped with the date and time. This is important to understand because your instructor will track your posts to make sure that they were submitted prior to each deadline.

Another feature is the ability to upload and access documents of all types. For example, your instructor will usually upload the following documents so that students can access them at any time: the course syllabus, lecture material, and any supplemental reading articles. With some software programs, you can also upload your own documents and save them in a digital file within a My Documents section of the program. That way, any documents that you create during the course can be stored on the college's secure server or network for easy access. Of course, you should always save your documents on your personal computer or portable device whenever possible. Yet if you ever find yourself on a public computer without any means to save your work, you can just save it directly in your online file, which is very convenient.

Finally, many software programs track and continuously calculate your overall grade as the course progresses. They will usually calculate test scores automatically, but your instructor will have to manually score the subjective areas of your performance (e.g., participation, papers, and group projects). As long as your instructor diligently inputs these scores, you should be able to access your current grade at any time. This is a nice feature because it allows you to track your progress in the course and know where you stand at any given moment.

In conclusion, online courses are growing in popularity in college academics today. You will likely take an online course at some point in your college career. Thus, it is imperative that you understand how online courses work and what is expected of you as a student. In this chapter, we discussed the various aspects of online courses and some of the things that you can do to set yourself up for success.

In the next chapter, we will consider what you should do if all else fails.

Key Points:

- At some point in your college career, you will probably find yourself enrolled in an online course.

- In order to succeed in online courses, you must be well-organized, disciplined, and motivated.

- Submit academically oriented message posts in a timely and respectful manner to receive maximum points for participation.

- Communication is absolutely essential in order to do well on group projects in online courses.

- Do not wait until the last minute to submit assignments, as unforeseen computer glitches can and do occur.

- Learn the dynamics of each software program, specifically the features that will help keep you on track and set you up for success.

CHAPTER 11:

If All Else Fails

If you have attempted some of the aforementioned tips, tools, and strategies but still seem to be struggling with a particular area of academics, do not panic. Help is available! Some conspiracy theorists might claim that colleges secretly want their students to struggle because then it takes them longer to graduate, which generates more revenue for the colleges. This could not be further from the truth.

Believe it or not, colleges *want* their students to succeed. After all, if colleges consistently have high dropout rates, it hurts not only their reputation but their bottom line as well. Moreover, it can negatively affect their accreditation status. Consequently, colleges have various resources on hand to help struggling students get the assistance they need, and there are several avenues that students can take to obtain this assistance.

Tutors

First and foremost, most colleges have tutors available to work with students who are struggling in certain courses. Tutors usually review course material with these students and help them get ready for tests. Some colleges have programs that provide tutors at no cost to students. Often, upper-level students who have demonstrated mastery of specific courses and are applying to graduate schools volunteer their time as tutors. Doing so helps strengthen their graduate school applications and prepare them for graduate school entrance exams. So you might be able to get help from one of these volunteer tutors for free.

Indeed, you could also hire a tutor on your own. Some students work as paid tutors on a part-time basis to earn supplemental income. Still, this usually costs quite a bit of money, especially if you meet with the tutor for the duration of the semester or school year. Most new college students cannot afford yet another expense on top of the hefty sums they are already paying for tuition, room and board, books, fees, and so forth.

Either way, if you do decide to use tutors, you will probably meet with them once or twice a week to review any material that you need help with at that time. You will also want to meet with them right before tests to clarify any information that you are unsure about. Regardless of how often you meet, understand that tutors are valuable resources that should not be wasted. Therefore, be sure to show up for all appointments and follow the tutors' advice closely, as they are the subject matter experts and know what they are talking about.

Study Groups

A student-organized study group is another option that might be available to you. Members of these groups are regular students who prefer to study with other students to help facilitate their own understanding and mastery of course material. You will find that most of the students in these groups are very willing to help others who might be struggling with any course material. Student-organized study groups are almost always free and usually meet around campus in the common areas of the dorms or at the school library. Ask around to see if any are available at your college and pay close attention to the flyers posted around campus, as study groups are often advertised in this manner.

Math/Science Lab

In terms of getting assistance with specific courses, there are a couple of options available. Most colleges offer a math lab and a science lab, where students can go to get help with courses that fall within these disciplines. Some colleges even offer labs or workshops specific to a particular course, such as calculus or physics. In any case, an instructor or TA is usually available to answer questions, as are upper-level students who have mastered the course material. Labs and workshops are open during specified times throughout the week and are usually free. Thus, if you want some additional assistance, be sure to make the most of these resources if they are available to you.

The Writing Workshop

For students who find that they are struggling with the writing process, nearly every college has some type of writing lab or writing workshop. The writing workshop is generally staffed by upper-level students who are very proficient writers. In fact, most students who work in the writing workshop are either English or journalism majors. Therefore, they are more than qualified to help other students who are having trouble with the writing process.

The staff in the writing workshop will typically provide one-on-one assistance to students. Yet do not make any false assumptions: they will not write your paper for you. Conversely, they will help you formulate an outline and generate ideas to get you started on the right path. They will even take the time to proofread your paper and provide constructive feedback on ways to improve it. Overall, I believe that this is one of the very best resources available to college students. Even if you consider yourself to be a pretty good writer, you will benefit from utilizing the writing workshop.

Library Resources

Finally, I would like to mention a few things to consider when gathering research. A multitude of campus resources are available to help students conduct research for papers and projects. Most noteworthy are the campus libraries and library staff. Get to know both very well. The campus libraries are staffed with highly trained individuals who can help you locate just about any type of resource you may want to include in your work. The library staff can help you find local resources, both in print and online, and can also process requests for items that are not available locally.

I like to think of librarians as the *keepers of knowledge*. They are specifically trained and cross-trained as research librarians, reference librarians, and archivists. They can help you find something in a matter of minutes that would have taken you hours to locate on your own. Therefore, do not be afraid to approach and ask them for help. They love helping students!

Online Databases

Along the same lines, you need to become familiar with the online databases and tools that your college offers. Prior to the digital age, students had to actually go to the library and find every piece of research in printed form in the library's "stacks," where scientific journals and other reference materials were kept. You can still do this at many colleges, but most of them are working toward scanning all of their resources and uploading them to databases so they can be used as digital media as well. Consequently, you should be able to locate a great deal of your research online via your college's library web page.

College libraries invest a significant amount of time and resources to scan and upload their local holdings into digital databases. They also pay a great deal of money to subscribe to various online research databases, such as EBSCOhost and CINAHL. These databases are gateways to literally thousands of scholarly journals, books, and other reference materials. In addition to being very convenient, online research databases are great because you can filter your searches to find exactly what you are looking for. You can also request items that are not available locally to be delivered to your college library.

Accessing online databases will save you a tremendous amount of time and aggravation when you go to conduct research. Learning how to use them is as easy as taking a brief class at your school library or simply asking a librarian for a quick tutorial. During your class or tutorial, you will be given a user name and password that will allow you to access the databases. Then, you should be well on your way to gathering valuable research for your papers and projects.

In conclusion, if you discover that you need some extra assistance with academics, do not fret. Numerous resources are available on campus to help you succeed. Knowing about these resources and how to use them is half the battle, so I hope this information will serve you well as you go about conquering the world of college academics!

Key Points:

- If you are struggling with a particular area of academics, do not panic. Help is available!

- Some colleges have programs that provide tutors at little or no cost to students.

- Study groups are a great way to network with your peers and to get some extra help mastering course content.

- Most colleges offer math and science labs, as well as writing workshops to assist students.

- Get to know your local librarians, as they can help you locate just about any piece of research you will ever need.

- Utilize online research databases: they will save you a tremendous amount of time and aggravation as you go about collecting research.

Chapter 12:
Stay Active and Have Fun

Now that we have discussed several specific topics pertaining to college academics, I would like to address a few holistic things that will affect your success in college.

An old adage goes, "A healthy body promotes a healthy mind." This is absolutely correct in many ways. As you well know, college academics can be very demanding and stressful. Failing to manage this stress can lead to negative outcomes, both in your professional life as a student and in your personal life as a spouse, sibling, parent, or child. Consequently, it is imperative to alleviate some of that stress by staying active and exercising on a regular basis.

Exercise is a natural way to relieve stress and tension throughout your body. It produces endorphins, which are the body's natural opioids. Exercise can also promote socialization via college athletics, intramurals, or aerobics, and there is no doubt that exercise contributes significantly to overall health and wellness. Thus, no matter how, when, or where you exercise, make it part of your weekly routine so that the stress of college academics does not get the best of you.

The other thing to remember about college academics is that you need to take some time to enjoy yourself. You will get burned out very quickly if all you ever do is study. Do not get me wrong:

succeeding in college academics means investing a considerable amount of time studying, but you need to have some fun as well. Try to set aside a block of time each day for recreation, and treat yourself after doing well on a big test or completing a paper or project.

While you are studying, take occasional study breaks. Spend a few minutes with your friends, watch part of a movie, or play a game. Study breaks give your mind time to rest and help keep you motivated to succeed because they disrupt the monotony of studying. Once you return to studying after a break, set a reasonable stopping point for the day. As previously stated, studying while you are fatigued is a waste of time because you will not retain much of the information.

As for the bigger picture, try to maintain a healthy balance between your academic life, your personal life, and your social life. Having too much or too little of any one of these aspects of your life will be a barrier to your success in college academics. So study hard, but do not lose sight of the bigger picture. Spend time with your family and friends, and always remember why (and for whom) you are working so hard to earn your college degree. In the end, all of the degrees, titles, and money in the world will mean nothing if you do not have anyone to share it with.

Key Points:

- Alleviate stress by staying active and exercising on a regular basis.

- Take time to enjoy yourself: set aside an hour each day for recreation.

- Take occasional study breaks to give your mind time to rest and to help keep you motivated to succeed.

- Try to maintain a healthy balance between your academic life, your personal life, and your social life.

Chapter 13:
Keep Your Eyes on the Prize

I mentioned earlier that the race to earn a college degree is a marathon, not a sprint. Therefore, you need to pace yourself: stay in the present and work toward completing smaller steps of the race along the way. For instance, do not overwhelm yourself by dwelling on how long it is going to take you to complete your degree. Conversely, think about the current semester and work toward specific goals as you go.

In addition, it is important to take time to reflect once you reach each milestone (i.e., the midterm, the end of the semester, and the end of the year). If you did not perform as well as you would have liked in one particular area or another, figure out ways to improve. If you exceeded what you thought you were capable of doing, pat yourself on the back for a job well done.

Either way, keep your eyes on the prize: your college degree. It might not seem like it when you are a freshman or a sophomore, but the time will go by faster than you think, so enjoy the ride while it lasts. Before you know it, you will be getting ready for graduation and filling out job applications!

Key Points:

- College is a marathon, not a sprint. Pace yourself and work toward completing smaller steps of the race along the way.

- Reflect upon your successes and your failures, and always seek to improve.

- College will go by faster than you think, so enjoy the ride while it lasts.

CHAPTER 14:
Life After College

Congratulations! You have graduated from college and earned that coveted college degree that you worked so hard to get. Not only did you finish the marathon, but you did so in grand fashion! Now what?

Well, there are many options available to you now that you are a college graduate. You could obviously get a job and go right to work, or you might consider going on to graduate school. In either case, the ultimate goal is to utilize your education so that you can get a good job.

Believe it or not, you can apply many of the tips, tools, and strategies presented in this book to your life after college as well. Discipline, motivation, punctuality, time management, organizational skills, and the effective utilization of available resources were just a few of the key things that I discussed in this book. Guess what? These are also many of the qualities that employers look for in new college graduates and in potential employees.

At this time, I am not going to review how to write a résumé or how to conduct yourself in a job interview, as there is a plethora of literature on these topics already. The point I want to emphasize is that you will be hired based upon your qualifications and your potential to perform. Although you are finished with college and will no longer receive actual letter grades anymore, you will still receive annual or semiannual evaluations from your employers.

An **evaluation report** documents your performance over a specified period and is used to measure your future potential. Just like during your college career, how you perform on a day-to-day basis will determine whether or not you receive a good "grade" (i.e., evaluation). Receiving good evaluations is very important because they are used to determine pay raises, benefits, and of course, promotions.

So keep this in the back of your mind as you land that first job and start working. The attitude, work ethic, and skill set that you develop in college will carry over into your life afterward. Thus, it is crucial for you to get on the right path early on in your college career. Your success, both during and after college, will depend upon it.

Key Points:

- You can apply many of the tips, tools, and strategies presented in this book to your life after college as well.

- Discipline, motivation, punctuality, time management, organizational skills, and the effective utilization of available resources are many of qualities that employers look for in potential employees.

- Although you are finished with college and will no longer receive actual letter grades anymore, you will still receive annual or semiannual evaluations from your employers.

- An evaluation report documents your performance over a specified period and is used to measure your future potential. It is also used to determine pay raises, benefits, and promotions.

Closing Remarks

In this book, I outlined numerous tips, tools, and strategies that I utilized throughout my college career to "ace" college. I realize that not every student desires to achieve a perfect 4.0 GPA. For some, a 3.5 or a 3.0 is more than sufficient. Still others just want to do enough to graduate and get their degrees. Whatever your goal is, I hope that this book has been informative and that it will benefit you in your journey through college academics.

By no means is this book all inclusive or *the only way* to succeed in college academics. Conversely, I merely attempted to expose you to the many different strategies and resources that you can draw upon to maximize your potential for academic success in college. You owe it to yourself to do the very best that you can with the opportunity that you have been given to earn a college education. Only a small percentage of the people in this world are fortunate enough to have the opportunity to go to college, so do not take it for granted.

Besides simply doing well in college academics, I hope you will use the information provided in this book to become more proficient in your chosen field of study. In doing so, you will have the chance to land a great job and begin to achieve all of your dreams. After all, education is a major ticket to success. Although one does not necessarily need a college education to make it in this world, it sure makes life a lot easier. Having a college education will open many doors for you over the course of your life and will significantly increase your earning power.

Yet perhaps the best part of getting a college education is knowing that you will be a well-informed citizen with a variety of experiences who understands more about the world than just your immediate surroundings. You will be able to speak intelligently about a wide range of topics, and regardless of what happens in your life, nobody will ever be able to take away your college degree or the knowledge that you gained while earning it.

Thank you for taking the time to read this book, and I wish you the very best that life has to offer!

Sincerely,

Jeffrey Vaske

Appendix A: Ten More Academic Tidbits

1. Meet with your academic advisor before the start of each semester to get advice on the courses that you are required to take as part of your major. Ask specific questions about each course and make sure that your advisor outlines a plan that will allow you to graduate on time. If you are not satisfied with your advisor, you can request a new one by talking to the head of your respective academic department.

2. If you are undecided on a major, spend the first year or two completing the required core curriculum or elective courses. This way, you will have more time to decide what you want to study but will still be making progress toward your degree. Also, you will not get set back by switching majors early on in your college career.

3. When selecting your courses for each semester, try to gather some information on each of your potential instructors. Instructors are just like anything else in life: there are good ones, and there are bad ones. A good instructor can greatly enhance your college experience and motivate you to succeed, while a bad instructor can drag you down and make one semester seem like an eternity. Whether good or bad, most instructors have a reputation on campus. Therefore, ask around and try to determine who the better instructors are before you finalize your course schedule.

4. Never pay full price for any of your textbooks: look for deals at the campus bookstore or online. You can usually purchase used textbooks that are still in very good condition and serve the exact same purpose. You can also offer to buy textbooks from a friend who has already taken the course. In any case, a little extra effort on your part will save you a great deal of money over the span of your college years.

5. Do not burn any GPA bridges: you might not have any desire to attend graduate school now, but you never know what the future might hold. Five, ten, or even fifteen years down the road, you might find yourself applying for graduate school and wishing you had a better GPA to put on your application. Thus, set a high academic standard for yourself right away during your freshman year and try to maintain it for the duration of your college career.

6. Along the same lines, it is important that you do the best you can in each course. Strive to earn all As and Bs, and do not settle for mediocrity. The popular phrase "Ds get degrees" is not entirely accurate, nor is it something to brag about. In fact, many academic programs require that you get a C or greater in each concentration course that is part of your declared major. Similarly, most professional programs require that you maintain a minimum of a 2.5 cumulative GPA. So in short, getting Ds will not serve you well. Understand how your school computes GPAs and know what you must earn in each course to remain in good academic standing within the institution.

7. Never take an "incomplete" for any course unless it is absolutely necessary for personal reasons. Withdrawing from a course after the deadline or taking an incomplete will drastically set you back.

Moreover, if you fail to complete the course at a later time, it will show up on your official college transcript, and you will automatically receive an F for that course. Receiving an F for any reason at any time in college will devastate your cumulative GPA, and you will spend the rest of your academic career trying to recover from it.

8. Approach your daily schedule in college academics like you would any job and if you put forth maximum effort during the day, then you should be able to enjoy the evening. For example, if you have three classes spread out over an eight-hour period, do not simply go back to your dorm room and watch television or sleep between those classes. Instead, use that free time to get your homework done. Go to the library or find a quiet place to study so that you can complete all of your homework during the day and enjoy the evening.

9. If you are in an associate's degree program, strive to get your bachelor's degree someday. Likewise, if you are in a bachelor's degree program, strive to earn your master's degree one day. In the current job market, a bachelor's degree is becoming almost like an associate's degree. In other words, more and more employers are seeking master's-prepared employees. Hence, in order to be more competitive in the job market, you will need as much education as possible.

10. Upon graduation, request an official copy of your final transcript and keep it in a safe place. You might have to provide a copy to an employer to verify when or where your degree was conferred. During the initial employment phase, transcripts will also be used for the credentialing process in many specialized fields (e.g., legal, medical, business, and so forth).

Appendix B: Poem and Prayer

by

Jeffrey Vaske

Fallen Soldier Tribute

Here lies a Soldier finally home from war
His weapon is silent, he fights no more
A twenty-one gun salute now honors thee
Who sacrificed everything so we could be free

Prayer of Thanksgiving

Dear Lord,

Thank you for the many gifts, talents, and blessings you have bestowed upon me. Please continue to bless not only me but my family and friends as well with good health, love, and happiness. I ask this through your Name.

    Amen

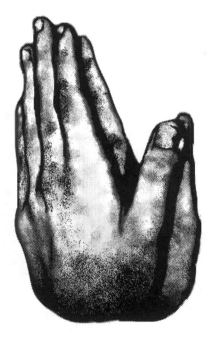

Appendix C: Reference List

1. "Using Your ACT Results," The ACT, 2010, accessed September 22, 2010, http://www.actstudent.org/pdf/uyar.pdf.

2. Dee Wright (Drake University), in discussion with the author, October 2002.

3. Christina Chang Wei, *What Is the Price of College? Total, Net, and Out-of-Pocket Prices in 2007–08* (Washington: US Department of Education, National Center for Education Statistics, 2010), 1, NCES 2011-175.

4. Constance Staley, *FOCUS on College Success*, 2d ed. (Boston: Wadsworth Cengage Learning, 2010), 263.

5. Kate L. Turabian, *A Manual for Writers of Research Papers, Theses, and Dissertations*, 7th ed., ed. Wayne C. Booth, Gregory G. Colomb, and Joseph M. Williams (Chicago: University of Chicago Press, 2007), xi.

6. Patrik Jonsson, "Is Eating Out Cheaper Than Cooking?" *The Christian Science Monitor*, 2006, accessed May 9, 2010, http://articles.moneycentral.msn.com/SavingandDebt/SaveMoney/IsEatingOutCheaperThanCooking.aspx.

7. "Plagiarism," Merriam-Webster.com, accessed January 10, 2011, http://www.merriam-webster.com/dictionary/plagiarize.

8. "Fast Facts," US Department of Education, National Center for Education Statistics, 2008, accessed January 11, 2011, http://nces.ed.gov/fastfacts/display.asp?id=80.

*In the Fallen Soldier Tribute, the word *Soldier* can be interchanged with *Sailor, Airman,* or *Marine.* Also, the words *his* and *he* can be interchanged with *her* and *she.*